107 SECRETS TO SUCCESS FOR THE GRADUATE

107 SECRETS TO SUCCESS FOR THE GRADUATE

Compiled

By

E. Aly

St. Simons Island, Georgia

© 2019 Marshwinds Press Company

All rights reserved. No part of this book may be reproduced or transmitted in any form or by any means, electronic or mechanical, including photocopying, recording, or by any information storage and retrieval system, except in the case of brief quotations embodied in critical articles and reviews, without prior written permission of the publisher.

Group sales are available by contacting:
Marshwinds Press Company
PO Box 21099
St. Simons Island, GA 31522
1-800-343-3751

Or go to uniquereads.com.

Library of Congress Control Number: 2019915482

ISBN Hardcover: 978-0-9614496-3-6
ISBN Paperback: 978-0-9614496-7-4
ISBN epub: 978-0-9614496-8-1

Interior design: Creative Publishing Book Design
All photos: Copyright by Marshwinds Press

For Judy
who understands success

CONGRATULATIONS!

You have achieved a significant milestone in your life. It was not easy—even if you made it look so. The path you have chosen for building your life's dreams has many challenges. There are definite steps for ensuring success.

Defining success—as you see it—points you to the right path. Many people have told you what their version of success is, hoping you will follow the path they chose for you. Thank them for their care and concern; however, assure them you are going to develop and design your own goals and objectives. Understand that the definition of success is going to change as you add life's experiences, reach milestones along the way, and build your life's wisdom.

HOW TO USE THIS BOOK

There are very few words in this book for a reason: It is not to be read once and put on a shelf. It is a book for your purse, satchel, or backpack. It is one you should read regularly, in snatches, when you are in line at the bank; waiting for a table at a restaurant; or riding in a car, bus, or train. This book is your road map for navigating life's challenges. The four sections build upon one another, like the foundation for any journey, to assist you with the inevitable twists, turns, ups, downs, and detours that are part of the life experience.

The best way to reap the fastest, smoothest, and most effective rewards from this guide are to do the following:

Step One: Have a pencil or pen in hand when reading. Start at the beginning with the "Attitude" section. As you read the secrets, be cognizant of which ones are most relevant to you at that moment. This relevancy can be either positive—a certain attitude you have now—or negative, some attitude you are lacking. Select the three secrets you feel are critical to you; and mark them #1, #2, and #3.

Step Two: Go through the "Courage" and "Work Ethics" sections the same way you did with the "Attitude" section. Don't forget to prioritize your top three secrets in each section.

Step Three: There are only 12 secrets in the "Communication" section. After reading through them, prioritize all 12 as far as how important they are to you at the moment you first read them.

Step Four: You have now begun personalizing the secrets. When you choose to reread them, start with whatever section you feel is important to you at that time. After selecting the section, go to the secrets you prioritized. Read them first, then start at the beginning of the section and read the rest. If another secret has increased relevancy for you because of your experiences with work, school, family, or friends, put it in the priory line (#4, #5, and so on). Change the order of what is important to you if you feel that one secret has gained in priority. Remember, this is your road map to success.

Step Five: The more you use the secrets, and the more your life experiences build, you will find that one section or another holds your interest to a greater extent. Start with that particular section, since you and your subconscious feel it is the most relevant. Then go to the other sections. This drawing of your interest to specific sections is proof that you are internalizing the truisms and using them. Your feelings of confidence and your ability to do what is necessary to succeed will grow and deepen the more times you read and think about these steps for achieving success. They will make a difference in your life. Try them. They work.

LIFE'S WISDOM

Building life's wisdom comes first from experience. Knowing and applying early in life certain success secrets will assist you in navigating the obstacles and opportunities on the success path you have chosen.

The 107 SECRETS TO SUCCESS in this book are tried-and-true ways to find the shortest path to achieving your goals. You will build your life's accomplishments on a solid foundation.

Each of these 107 SECRETS TO SUCCESS has originated in history. Most were spoken by someone who understands success. All came from life's experiences. The progression and linking of the secrets are important. By interlocking the knowledge, you will build a solid foundation as you move forward up the success path.

Only a few people achieve true success during their life. Why? Because success takes the proper *attitude, courage, work ethics,* and *communication.* As you read these pages, think about, understand, and implement these truisms for the ages.

107 SECRETS TO SUCCESS FOR THE GRADUATE

ATTITUDE

In the 1600s, attitude meant the posture of a figure in a sculpture and painting. The word evolved to mean not only a physical attitude, but a mental "posture" as well. Today it means the way a person thinks about opportunities, challenges, and life in general. Your attitude will filter unexpected challenges and opportunities from life and your subconscious.

On September 11, 2001, the United States and New York City sustained an enormous blow from the terror attacks on the World Trade Center towers. The unexpected destruction of human life, property values, and damage to the psychological security of citizens could have left the country paralyzed. It didn't. The deep-seated *attitude* of the country, the city, and the citizens did not allow it. Today, the devastated area has been reborn, even better than it was, as a testament to the positive attitude of this country.

Without the proper attitude, you will never succeed at anything except failure, so remember:

1

If you want to know
the future, create it.

2

Happiness in life comes from
loving and being loved.

3

Optimism is the key
to leadership.

4

We are not interested in the
possibility of defeat.

QUEEN VICTORIA

Attitude

He who has a why to live
can bear with almost any how.

FRIEDRICH NIETZSCHE

Life is worth less than the moments
of being alive.

Believe you can and you
are halfway there.

THEODORE ROOSEVELT

No matter how dark the future
may seem, there is still light in the
present to give happiness.

Absorbing the excitement and mystery
of the world is part of being alive.

10

Upon waking up in the morning,
think three positive thoughts.

11

The best way to find out if you
can trust someone is to trust them.

12

Wake up looking forward to embracing
the new and different.

13

The only easy day was yesterday.

U.S. NAVY SEAL MOTTO

14

Giving up is the ultimate tragedy.

15

Focus on your goal and ignore
all other distractions.

Attitude

16

Common sense is not common.

VOLTAIRE

17

You can't control what others do or say, but you control 100% of how you react.

18

Only listen to those who give factual and blunt advice.

19

For every minute you are angry, you lose 60 seconds of happiness.

RALPH WALDO EMERSON

20

Life is precious. Spend time every day broadening your knowledge of life.

21

Six leadership traits: curiosity, courage, perseverance, integrity, confidence, and empathy.

SUN TZU

22

Nothing worthwhile is worth doing halfway. Commit to full effort or walk away.

23

Define success as the ability to be proud of who you see when looking in the mirror.

24

Nothing is impossible. The word itself says *I'm possible*.

25

Don't assume anything because if you do, you make an *ass-(of)-u-(and)-me*.

Attitude

26

Success is a consequence
and must not be an end.

GUSTAVE FLAUBERT

27

It is often merely for an excuse that
we say things are impossible.

FRANCOIS DE LA ROCHEFOUCAULD

28

A person who dares to waste one hour
of time has not discovered the value of life.

CHARLES DARWIN

29

Dress every day believing you will be seen
by the most important person you know.

30

The first important factor in
success is attitude.

31

If you want to know who is keeping you from success, look in the mirror.

32

The road to success is not straight. There are many twists, turns, and detours, so enjoy the entire journey.

33

Always surround yourself with friends and associates who are smarter than you.

34

Never be afraid to allow your boss to get the credit for your job well done.

35

In your life and work, be a warrior, not a whiner.

36

Do what you're passionate about, understanding your desires evolve as you mature. In this way, you will always be successful.

37

If you don't believe in yourself, no one else will believe in you.

38

People respond to what they receive, so be positive.

39

Joy at endeavors makes success come more often.

40

You can't recognize and appreciate good times without having experienced bad times.

COURAGE

When thinking of first responders and soldiers who answer their country's call to duty, it's easy to see courage on display. Incorrectly, from an early age, we equate courage with fearlessness. This is wrong. Courageous individuals are not fearless; they have the same fears we all do. They understand, however, they must embrace their fears to accomplish what they want in life.

Courage is not exclusive to individuals in high-risk situations. Correctly walking any path of life takes courage. Every day a single parent faces fears of raising a child alone. Every semester a student faces the challenges of new subjects and instructors. Small business owners fear a loss of business. Employees fear their jobs will not be secure for any period. Everyone faces fears every day. You are not unique in your anxieties. Overcoming those fears is courage, so remember:

41

Where you are is merely the starting
point and irrelevant to where you end up.

42

A Creed for Life
Dear God . . .
Give me the knowledge to know what I
need to do.
Give me the courage to do what I
know needs to be done.
Give me the strength to keep moving
through the valleys.
And, dear God . . .
Help me realize that if I wake up
in the morning breathing,
and my mind can realize that fact,
You have done Your part. The rest is up to me.

Courage

43

Courage is understanding
fear is normal and should be ignored
in times of stress.

44

Fortune favors the bold.

VIRGIL

45

Fear narrows your world.
Overcoming fear expands it.

46

We must dare, and dare again,
and go on daring.

GEORGES J. DANTON

47

Make your own luck.

USSF MOTTO

48

Necessity is the mother
of taking chances.

MARK TWAIN

49

Where there is a will, there is a way.

50

Forces opposed to change do not give
up easily. Steady, consistent persuasion
is necessary to win.

51

The harder the conflict, the more
glorious the triumph.

THOMAS PAINE

52

It is never too late to begin the
journey to success.

53

Keep your fears to yourself,
but share your courage
with others.

ROBERT LOUIS STEVENSON

54

Act as if what you do makes a
difference. It does.

WILLIAM JAMES

WORK ETHICS

There are multitudes of intelligent and perceptive people who never achieve success in their life. Some of them have the right attitude and courage. Why? Just as plentiful are individuals who are challenged intellectually, yet they seem to always achieve their goals. Why?

The path to success has many twists, turns, ups, downs, and detours. To stay the course requires the discipline and work ethics for going the distance, so remember:

To know your limit in
anything, find it.

56

What you hear does not stay.
What you see lingers.
What you do remains.

57

Do an action every day
for 21 days and it becomes a habit.
Habits break
after missing one day.

58

The eye of the master
will do more work
than both of his hands.

BEN FRANKLIN

59

Fast is fine,
but accuracy is everything.

XENOPHON

Work Ethics

60

Compounding small disciplined
steps leads to success.

61

No journey is too great
if you find what you seek.

62

Don't try to rush success.
Calmly accumulate small triumphs
and build a strong foundation daily.

63

Fall seven times and
stand up eight.

64

I'm a great believer in luck,
and I find the harder I work,
the more I have of it.

THOMAS JEFFERSON

65

Can you imagine
what I would do
if I could do all I can?

SUN TZU

66

Career ladders are climbed
one rung at a time,
with success growing geometrically.

67

Only you are responsible
for your actions,
and actions have consequences,
both good and bad.

68

Learning without thought
is labor lost.

CONFUCIUS

69

I have not failed. I've just
found 10,000 ways that won't work.

THOMAS EDISON

70

Do what you can, with what
you have, where you are.

THEODORE ROOSEVELT

71

Stretch into the unknown in your
profession in order to grow and thrive.

72

Genius is eternal patience.

MICHELANGELO

73

True education begins
when leaving school and experiencing life.
Study life's wonders to learn success.

74

Always make time every day
to sit quietly and think.

75

The beginning is the most
important part of the work.

PLATO

76

There is no substitute for hard work.

THOMAS EDISON

77

We are what we repeatedly do.
Excellence, then, is not an act, but a habit.

ARISTOTLE

78

It does not matter how slowly you
go as long as you do not stop.

CONFUCIUS

79

Great things are done by a series of small things brought together.

VINCENT VAN GOGH

80

Master your profession in order to change it effectively for greater success.

81

The most certain way to success is always to try just one more time.

THOMAS EDISON

82

It is better to fail at originality than to succeed at imitation.

HERMAN MELVILLE

83

Thoughts lead on to purposes;
purposes go forth in actions;
actions form habits;
habits decide character;
and character
fixes destiny.

TRYON EDWARDS, THEOLOGIAN

84

Beware of missing chances;
otherwise, it may be
altogether too late
someday.

FRANZ LISZT

85

Do what is necessary
for success—
you know what it is
and what it takes.

Work Ethics

86

When you fail at a task,
take 60 seconds
to be upset with yourself,
and then take 60 minutes
to learn from your failure.

87

Do not cheat
in your profession.
If you do, you cheat yourself.

88

Reason and judgment are the
qualities of a leader.

TACITUS

89

A short saying oft contains
much wisdom.

SOPHOCLES

90

Better be wise
by the misfortune
of others than your own.

AESOP

91

Ambition can creep
as well as soar.

EDMUND BURKE

92

Probable impossibilities
are to be preferred
to improbable possibilities.

ARISTOTLE

93

Never look backwards
or you will
fall down the stairs.

RUDYARD KIPLING

94

Experience is the teacher
of all things.

JULIUS CAESAR

95

When it is difficult to make a decision,
decide what you believe is best,
wait one hour, and see how you feel
about your choice.

COMMUNICATION

Humans are lost without communication with others. Communication is a two-way process—giving and receiving information. From communication comes understanding, respect, and sharing. No matter what you want to accomplish in life, no matter what profession you choose, no matter if you have the right attitude, courage, and work ethics, unless and until you can communicate with those most important to your life's goals—family, friends, coworkers, or customers—you will fall short. This interaction with others is crucial, so remember:

96

Communication success
comes from two factors:
knowledge of subject
and motivation.

97

Vision is the art of seeing
things invisible.

JONATHAN SWIFT

98

Your customer is ***always right.***

99

Communication is perfectly imperfect,
so speak in a direct way.

100

The least significant idea in your communication
is as critical as the most significant
for building lasting success.

101

Build your own success
by satisfying others' wants and needs.

102

Ask for the customers' trust and confidence
and it will be given.

103

Customers do not buy
products, features, or advantages;
they buy benefits
for themselves.

104

Every person likes
to hear their own name.
Use it in communication
for more success.

105

Practice communication skills daily.

106

Short, open-ended questions
allow customers to communicate
their own wants, needs, and concerns.

107

When the communication goal
is reached, thank the customer
and politely disengage.

CONGRATULATIONS!

You now have the road map to success. No one can take this knowledge away from you. If you take 10 minutes in the morning (while eating breakfast) and 10 minutes at night (last thing before turning out the lights) to reread these jewels of wisdom, you will internalize the knowledge and find it resurfacing at the correct moment, helping you take the next step on your path to success.

ACKNOWLEDGEMENTS

The 107 Secrets to Success for the Graduate is the result of many helping hands. My assistant, Amy Sheree Adams, rose to the challenges of reading my handwriting and putting up with my tweaking the message almost daily.

Luke Palder and his staff at ProofreadingServices.com know better than anyone that I spent more time daydreaming in English classes than paying attention. They did a wonderful job making the manuscript readable.

Ghislain Viau, Creative Publishing Book Design, took the manuscript and developed an aesthetically pleasing and focused design. His talents resulted in a presentation that is crisp and free of distractions.

Jenna Smith and the staff at CGBOOK Printers for their patience and expertise.

Lastly, my wife and stalwart supporter, Judy, has always been my muse, allowing me to dream of what I wanted to accomplish, and then saying, "What are you waiting for? Do it." She understands success.

NOTES

NOTES

NOTES

www.ingramcontent.com/pod-product-compliance
Lightning Source LLC
Chambersburg PA
CBHW072114290426
44110CB00014B/1906